Awesome Pets

by
David Orme

Thunderbolts

Awesome Pets
by David Orme

Illustrated by Paul Boston

Published by Ransom Publishing Ltd.
Radley House, 8 St. Cross Road, Winchester, Hants. SO23 9HX, UK
www.ransom.co.uk

ISBN   978 178127 075 2
First published in 2013
Copyright © 2013 Ransom Publishing Ltd.

Illustrations copyright © 2013 Paul Boston
Micro pig photographs courtesy of pet piggies: www.petpiggies.co.uk.
'Get the Facts' section - images copyright: cover, prelims, passim – Pet Piggies, Stephan Czuratis; pp 4/5 - Alvesgaspar; pp 6/7 - Mike Russell, Erick Gómez Villalvazo, Dalius Baranauskas, Patricia Vicente, Tiefflieger; pp 8/9 - Pet Piggies, Guido Gerding, Brian Gratwicke; pp 10/11 - Dan Bennett, David Shankbone, Ltshears, Patricia Vicente, Eesterle, Abuk SABUK, Tomasz Wawak; pp 12/13 - Papooga, Brent Holland, Eric Isselée; pp 14/15 - Blaine Hansel, DanDee Shots, Ian Sane; pp 16/17 - M3xx; pp 18/19 - JJ Harrison, Andy Moser, Matthew Field, Ianaré Sévi; pp 20/21 - Michael Olson, Marcus Lindström, Pierre Fidenci; pp 22/23 - Ikiwaner, Alan Wilson, Nachoman-au, Luca Galuzzi, J. Petersen; p 36 - 4028mdk09.

A CIP catalogue record of this book is available from the British Library.

All rights reserved. No part of this publication may be reproduced, stored in a retrieval system, or transmitted, in any form or by any means, electronic, mechanical, photocopying, recording or otherwise, without the prior permission of the publishers.

The rights of David Orme to be identified as the author and of Paul Boston to be identified as the illustrator of this Work have been asserted by them in accordance with sections 77 and 78 of the Copyright, Design and Patents Act 1988.

Contents

Awesome Pets: The Facts   5

1. Pick your pet!   6
2. Pigs as pets   8
3. Dogs – all shapes and sizes!   10
4. Clever pets   12
5. Working pets   14
6. Animal heroes   16
7. Weird pets   18
8. Taking animals from the wild is bad …   20
9. The world's most dangerous pets   22

Marvin to the Rescue!   25

THUNDER BOLTS

4

Awesome Pets: The Facts

Pick your pet!

Guinea pig

Cat

Hamster

Goldfish

Dog

Pigs as pets

✓ Good as pets.

8

Not good as pets.

What about the mess?

They are easy to train – but do have accidents sometimes.

Dogs – all shapes and sizes

Grumpy dogs

Jumping dogs

Cute dogs

Sad dogs

Happy dogs

Posh dogs

Crazy dogs

Clever pets

Hi there. I know over 100 words. Let's talk!

I'm a baby. So I only know 9 words.

This is worse than being at school!

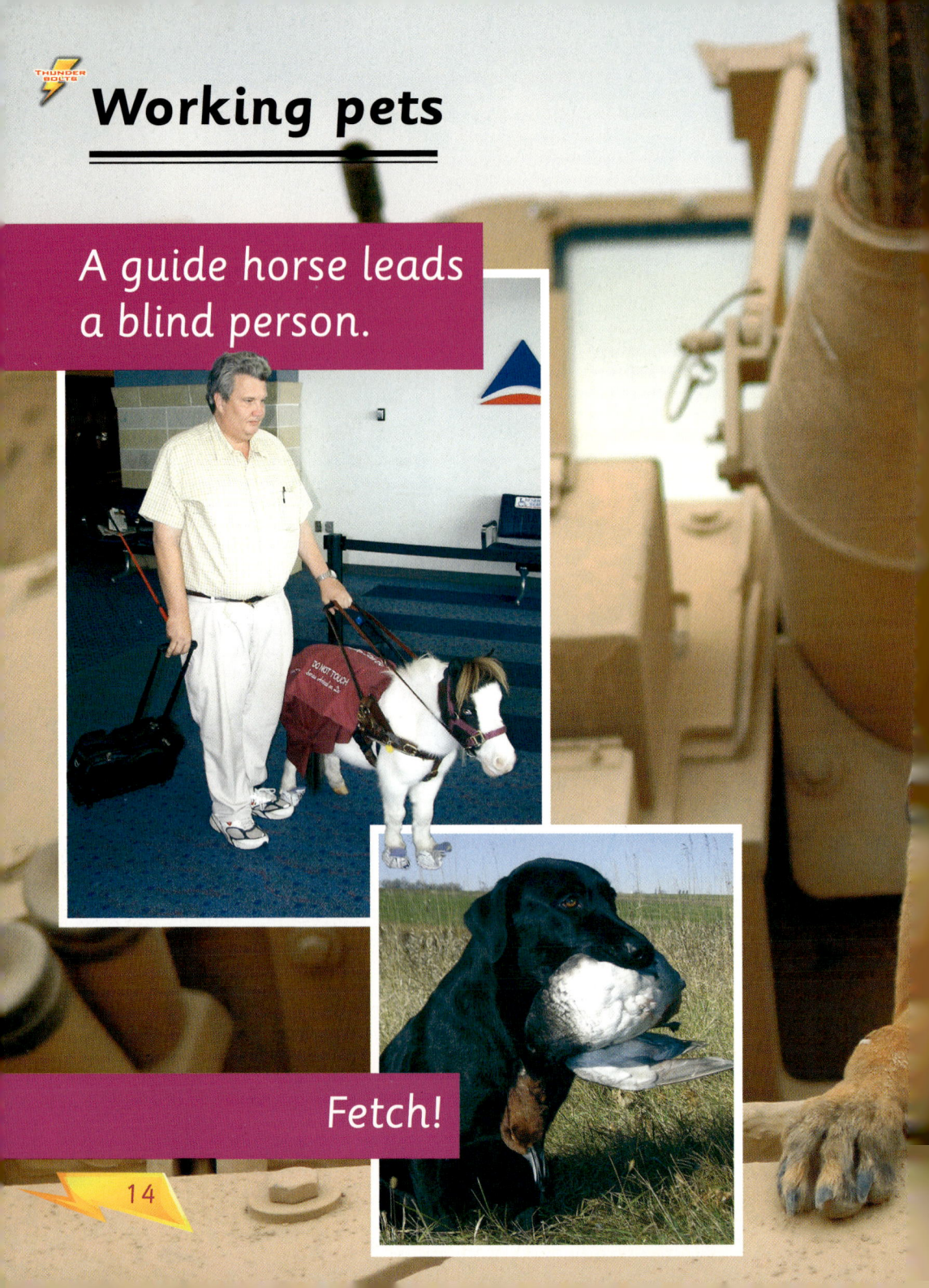

Working pets

A guide horse leads a blind person.

Fetch!

These dogs are making this scooter go!

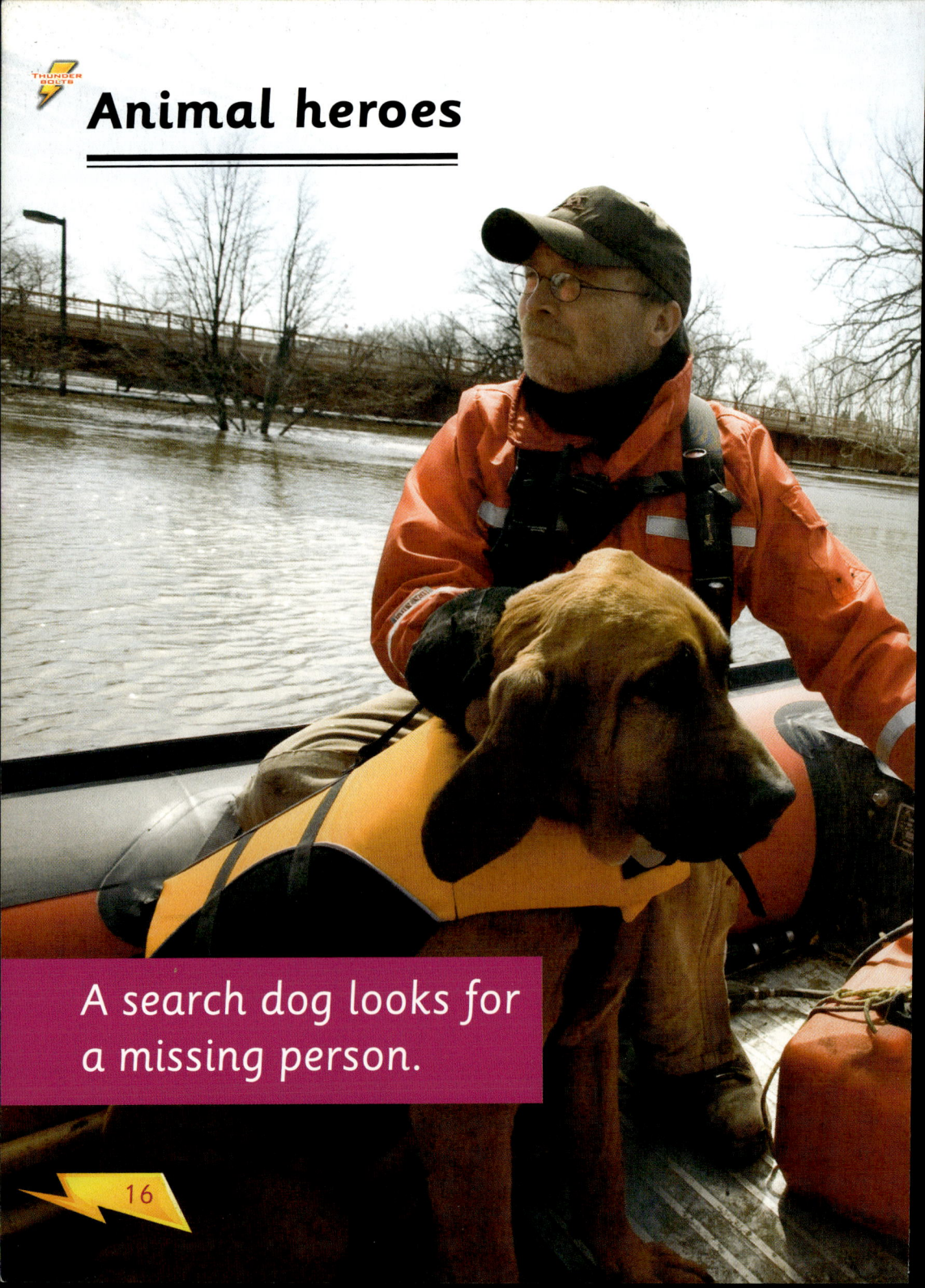

Animal heroes

A search dog looks for a missing person.

A war-time carrier pigeon.

A tired search dog has a rest.

Weird pets

Jumping spider

Hissing cockroach

18

Baby alligators look cute ...

... but what happens when they grow?

Taking animals from the wild is bad ...

Hunters may kill mothers to steal their babies.

Is this right or wrong?

Sold as pets ...

... and now nearly extinct.

The world's most dangerous pets

Would you like one of these for a pet?

The blue-ringed octopus. Very dangerous!

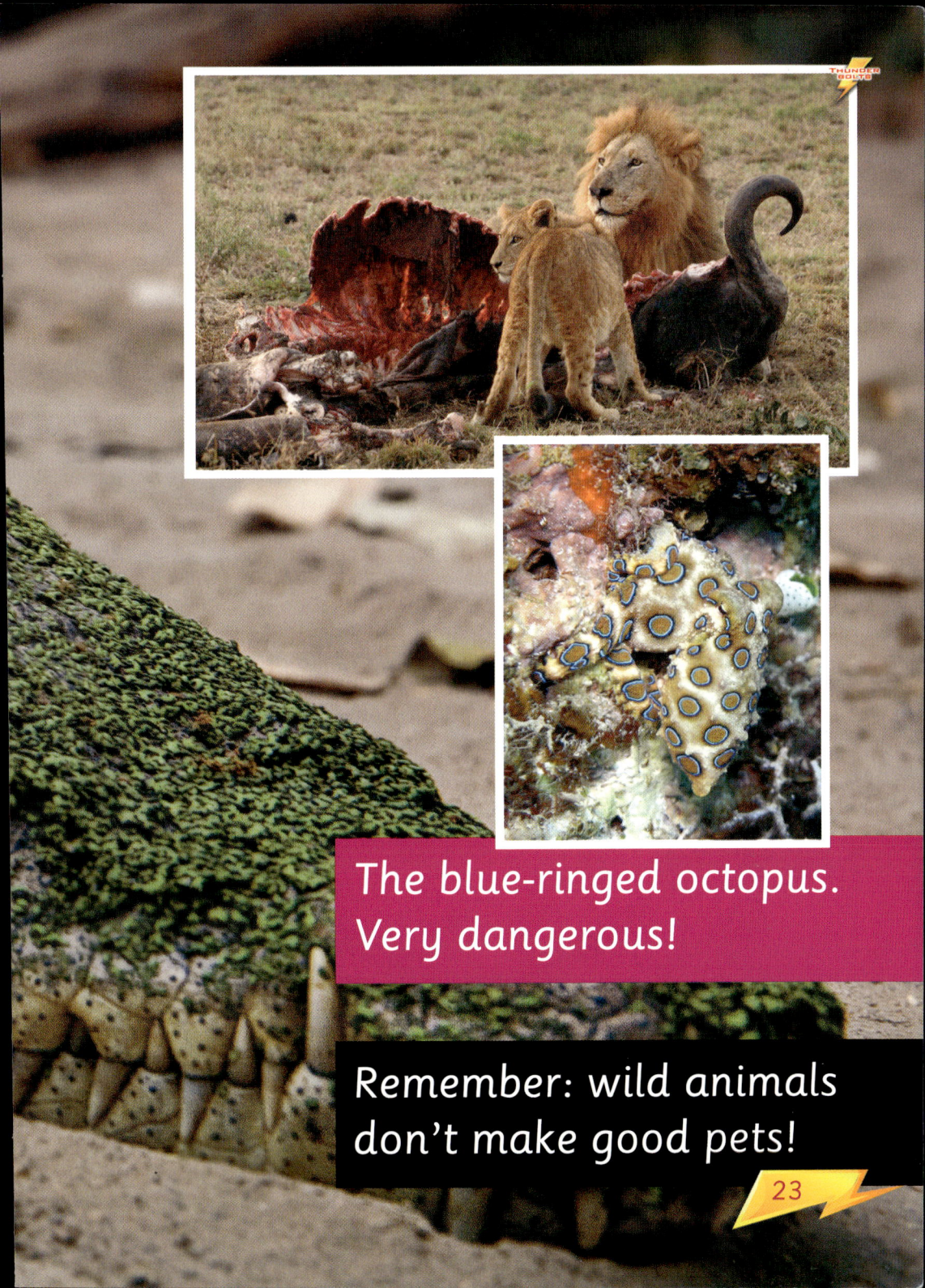

Remember: wild animals don't make good pets!

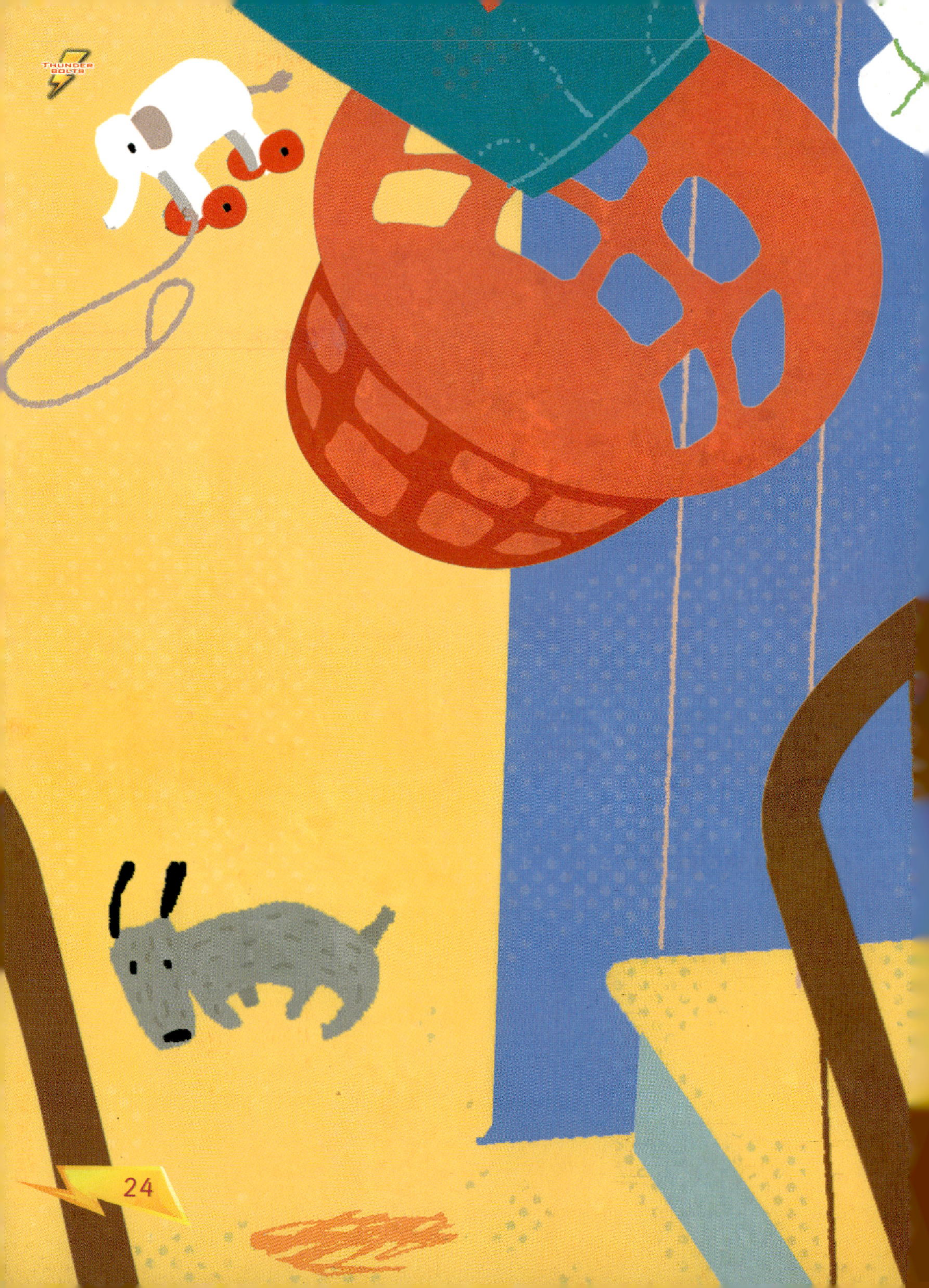

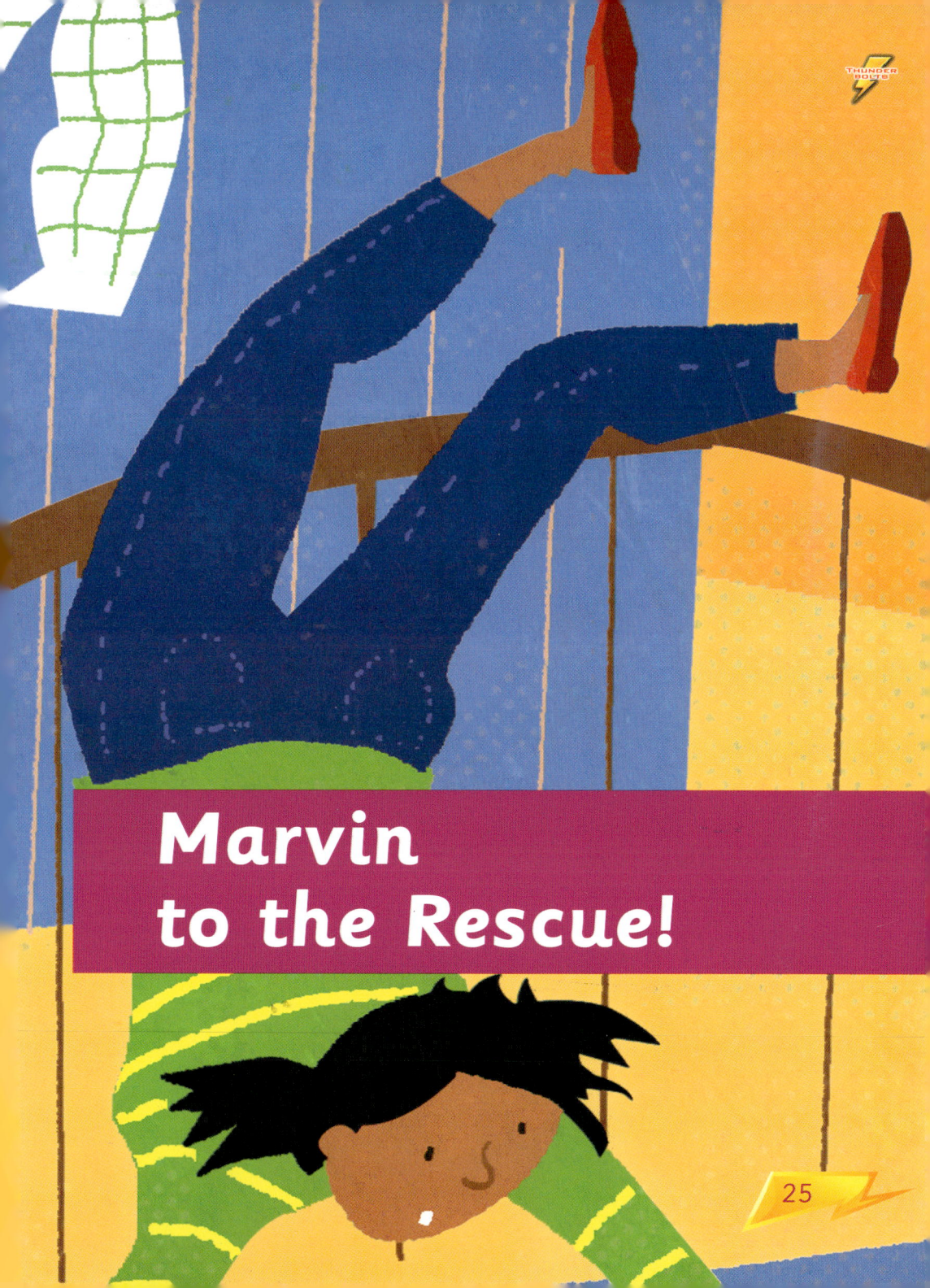

Marvin to the Rescue!

Look out, Mum!

I told you to look out!

27

Things are looking serious ...

H – help!

28

But Marvin's on the case!

Will anyone hear Marvin?

Woof! Woof!

There's no one to hear!
What can Marvin do?

Marvin's a smart dog!

"Marvin, you're a star!"

An ambulance has arrived …

You've broken your leg, I'm afraid.

The family are visiting Mum in hospital …

Marvin gets a medal!

Mum's leg is getting better.

What's going to happen next?

35

Word list

accident
alligator
ambulance
blind
carrier
clever
cockroach
crazy
cute
dangerous
extinct
fetch
fruit
guinea pig
heroes
octopus
pigeon
school
serious
shape
sometimes
train
weird
working